RUBANK

SOLO AND ENSEMBLE SERIES

Hungarian Dance No. 5

Johannes Brahms
arr. J.B. Quick and E. De Lamater

for MARIMBA or XYLOPHONE
with piano accompaniment

RUBANK®

Hal•Leonard®

Hungarian Dance No.5

Piano

JOH. BRAHMS
Score by E. De Lamater

Copyright, MCMXXXV, by Rubank, Inc., Chicago, Ill.
International Copyright Secured

Hungarian Dance No.5

Marimba
or Xylophone

JOH. BRAHMS
Arr. by John B. Quick
Xylophonist

Copyright MCMXXXV by Rubank Inc., Chicago, Ill.
International Copyright Secured

Piano

Hungarian Dance No.5

SNARE DRUM SOLOS Unaccompanied

HL04479337	Bobbin' Back (Buggert)	*Grade 4*
HL04479340	Echoing Sticks (Buggert)	*Grade 4*
HL04479345	Rolling Accents (Buggert)	*Grade 4*

MARIMBA/XYLOPHONE SOLOS with Piano Accompaniment

HL04479361	Ave Maria (Schubert/arr. Edwards) *Grade 2*
HL04479367	Flight of the Bumblebee (Rimsky-Korsakov/arr. Quick) *Grade 4*
HL04479368	Hungarian Dance No. 5 (Brahms/arr. Quick) *Grade 3*
HL04479372	Largo from New World Symphony (Dvořák/arr. Quick) *Grade 2.5*
HL04479374	Light Cavalry Overture (von Suppe/arr. Quick) *Grade 4.5*
HL04479475	March Militaire, Op. 51 No. 1 (Schubert/arr. Quick) *Grade 3.5*
HL04471140	Music for Marimba, Vol. 1 (2- or 3-mallet solos/duets with piano) (Jolliff) *Grade 1-2*
HL04471150	Music for Marimba, Vol. 2 (2- or 3-mallet solos with piano) (Jolliff) *Grade 2-3*
HL04471160	Music for Marimba, Vol. 3 (3- or 4-mallet solos with piano) (Jolliff) *Grade 3*
HL04479480	Rhapsodic Fantasie (Edwards/based on Liszt's *Hungarian Rhapsody No. 2*) *Grade 4*

DRUM ENSEMBLES Instrumentation as marked

HL04479349	Double Drummin' (two snares w/piano accompaniment) (Harr) *Grade 2*
HL04479351	Flinging It Threefold (trio for three snares) (Buggert) *Grade 2*
HL04479356	Ticonderoga (trio for two snares and bass) (Harr) *Grade 3*
HL04479359	We Three (trio for three snares) (Buggert) *Grade 3*

U.S. $7.99

HL04479368

RUBANK®

HAL•LEONARD®

7777 W. BLUEMOUND RD. P.O. BOX 13819 MILWAUKEE, WI 53213

ISBN-13: 978-1-4950-1477-2

Distributed By

HAL LEONARD

04479368